Sadlier Sacrament Program

With You Always

First Reconciliation

Dr. Gerard F. Baumbach
Moya Gullage

Rev. Msgr. John F. Barry
Dr. Eleanor Ann Brownell
Helen Hemmer, I.H.M.
Dr. Norman F. Josaitis
Rev. Michael J. Lanning, O.F.M.
Dr. Marie Murphy
Karen Ryan
Joseph F. Sweeney

with
Dr. Thomas H. Groome
Boston College

Official Theological Consultant
Most Rev. Edward K. Braxton, Ph. D., S.T.D.

Pastoral Consultant
Rev. Virgilio P. Elizondo, Ph. D., S.T.D.

Catechetical and Liturgical Consultants
Dr. Gerard F. Baumbach
Dr. Eleanor Ann Brownell

William H. Sadlier, Inc.
9 Pine Street
New York, NY 10005–1002

Nihil Obstat

✠Most Reverend George O. Wirz
Censor Librorum

Imprimatur

✠Most Reverend William H. Bullock
Bishop of Madison
July 10, 1995

Ⓢ is a registered trademark of William H. Sadlier, Inc.

Home Office:
9 Pine Street
New York, NY 10005-1002

ISBN: 0-8215-2401-1

26 27 28 29 30 31 32/12 11 10 09 08

Acknowledgments

Excerpts and adaptations from *Good News Bible*, copyright © American Bible Society 1966, 1971, 1976, 1979.

Excerpts from the English translation of *Rite of Penance* © 1974, International Committee on English in the Liturgy, Inc. (ICEL). All rights reserved.

"Always Ready to Forgive," © 1990, Carey Landry and North American Liturgy Resources (NALR). All rights reserved. "Let There Be Peace on Earth," © renewed 1983, 1955, Jan-Lee Music, Honokaa, Hawaii. All rights reserved. "God Has Made Us a Family," © 1986, Carey Landry and North American Liturgy Resources (NALR). All rights reserved. "We Come to Ask Forgiveness," © 1986, Carey Landry and North American Liturgy Resources. All rights reserved. "New Hope," © 1976, North American Liturgy Resources (NALR), 5536 NE Hassalo, Portland, OR 97213. All rights reserved. Used with permission. "Peace to You and Me," © 1986, Carey Landry and North American Liturgy Resources (NALR). All rights reserved.

Photo Credits

Jim Saylor   Mary Kate Coudal
Photo Editor   Photo Research

Cate Photography: 4, 5, 6, 7, 10, 11 right, 14, 15 top right, 18, 19 bottom, 21, 26, 34, 35, 42, 43, 46, 50–51, 54, 55.
CROSIERS/ Gene Plaisted, OSC: 18/19, 44/45.
Kathy Ferguson: 15 top left.
James Frank: 41 top.
Gerald French/ FPG International: 15 bottom.
Ken Karp: 11 left, 12, 20, 22, 23, 27, 28, 30/31, 31, 36.
H. Armstrong Roberts: 76 center.
Tony Stone Images/ Lori Adamski Peek: 19 top; Dan Bosler: 40 left; Ken Fisher: 76 top left, 76 bottom right; Bruce Aryes: 76 top right; Peter Correz: 76 bottom left.
Rod Walker: 41 bottom.
George White: 40 right.

Illustrators

Bonnie Matthews: 3, 4–8, 10–12, 14–16, 18–20, 22–24, 26–28, 30–32, 34–38, 40–46, 48, 50–51, 54–79
Robert VanNutt: 9, 17, 25, 33, 38–39, 49, 52, 57, 59, 61, 63.
65, 67, Jesus cutout
Michael Woo: 21, 29, 47, 53, pinwheel cutout

Contents

A Preparation Rite

Leader: Jesus says, "I am the Good Shepherd. I know My sheep and they know Me."

Based on John 10:15

All: (To the tune of "Did You Ever See A Lassie?")

♪ Oh, Jesus is our Friend, and our
Brother and Shepherd.
Jesus teaches us to love and to
follow His way.
In joy and in faith and in hope and
thanksgiving,
Jesus teaches us to love and to
follow His way. ♪

Leader: As a parish family, we welcome you as
you begin to prepare for the sacrament of
Reconciliation. We join with you as you get
ready to celebrate God's great love and
mercy. As followers of Jesus, the Good
Shepherd, we help each other by praying:

Leader: Jesus, help us to grow in faith and trust.
All: Jesus, Good Shepherd, hear us.
Leader: Jesus, help us to love and follow You.
All: Jesus, Good Shepherd, hear us.

Leader: Jesus, help us to share Your peace with others.

All: Jesus, Good Shepherd, hear us.

Leader: Parents, turn to your children and trace the sign of the cross on their foreheads.

Parents: Child of God, I sign you in the name of Jesus, the Good Shepherd, who will never leave you. Follow Him as He calls you to the sacrament of Reconciliation.

Leader: Children, please come forward holding your Good Shepherd figure. We will end our prayer by singing our song together.

All: (To the tune of "Did You Ever See a Lassie?")
♪ Oh, we are friends of Jesus, our
    Brother and Shepherd.
Jesus teaches us to love and to follow
    His way.
Our friends and our family will help
    us get ready.
For Your peace and Your forgiveness,
    dear Jesus, we pray. ♪

1 Following Jesus

You are growing up.
You are growing taller and stronger.
As a Catholic, you are also learning
to grow in love and understanding of
your faith.

Think for a minute.
Tell something you love or understand
about God the Father.
Tell something you love or understand
about Jesus, who is God the Son.
Tell something you love or understand
about God the Holy Spirit.

Soon you will celebrate the wonderful
sacrament of Reconciliation. Let's begin
our preparation time together.

✝ In the name of the Father,
and of the Son,
and of the Holy Spirit.
Amen.

Do you remember the story of the first people?
They disobeyed God. They sinned. Their sin
is called original sin. We are all born with
original sin. Baptism takes away original sin
and makes us God's children.

God gives us the gift of choice.
Choices are things we do on purpose.
We are free to choose to do what is right.
We can also choose to do what is wrong.

Today we are going to hear a story from the
Bible about someone who first made a wrong
choice and then made a right choice!

The Forgiving Father

There was a loving father who had two sons. One day the younger son said to his father: "Father, give me my share of the family money." He wanted to leave home and have some fun.

The father was very sad but he gave his son the money and watched him leave home.

At first the young man had a wonderful time. He gave parties and made many new friends. Soon, however, his money was gone. His friends left him. He was poor and homeless and hungry.

Now he began to think about the choice he had made. The son remembered his home and his father's great love for him!

The young man said:
"I will go home to my father. I will say, 'Father, I have sinned against God and against you. I am not fit to be your son. Treat me as one of your servants.'"

Then he began his long trip home.

His father kept hoping that one day his son would return. Each day he watched and waited. When he saw his son coming down the road, he ran to meet him and hugged him. Then the father said to his servants:

"Put the best robe on my son and new shoes on his feet. Now we will celebrate, for my son who was dead is alive again. He was lost, but now he's found!"

Based on Luke 15:11–24

What wrong choice did the son make?
What right choice did he make?
What choices did the father make?
What do you learn from this story about God's great love for us?

Making Loving Choices

Jesus showed us how to make good and loving choices. He was kind to others. He healed the sick. He forgave sins. He brought people peace. He taught us that love is the most important thing of all.

It is not always easy to make right and loving choices.

We should always begin by asking God to help us make the right choice in following Jesus. Then, if what we have to choose is hard or something serious, we need to talk about it with someone we trust — a parent or another grown-up. Then, with the help of the Holy Spirit, we choose the right and loving thing to do.

Sometimes what we do may cause a problem. We may make a mistake. We may do something by accident. Then it is not our fault. Mistakes and accidents are not sins.

How can you show you are Jesus' follower?
How can you make loving choices?

How to Make
a Loving Choice

1. Think about the choices you can make.

2. Ask yourself which choice Jesus would want you to make.

3. Talk to God about your choices. Ask the Holy Spirit to help you to choose to do right and loving things as Jesus did.

4. Talk over your choices with someone who can help you.

5. With the help of the Holy Spirit, make your choice.

What Is a Choice?

Read these stories. Work with a partner and label them W (a wrong choice), R (a right choice), A (an accident), or M (a mistake). Explain your answers.

▷ Luis did not do his math. He brought home his reader instead of his math book.

▷ Bonnie spilled spaghetti sauce on her sister's favorite sweater.

▷ Hal used his father's computer without permission to play a game with his friends.

▷ Tim and Corey were ready to fight but Angie helped them to shake hands instead.

Close your eyes. Be very still. Thank God for giving you the freedom to make choices. Ask God to help you to make loving choices that Jesus wants His friends to make.

12

At Home

Write the letter that matches each colored shape.

A	C	D	E	G	H	I	K	L	M	N	O	P	S	T	V	Y
●	■	◆	■	◀	▶	●	■	◀	■	◆	●	▶	●	◀	■	◆

1. We learn to C _ _ _ _ _ _ right from wrong.

2. We should ask God to _ _ _ _ _ _ _ us.

3. We want to choose _ _ _ _ _ things to do as Jesus did.

4. Sometimes we make _ _ _ _ _ _ _.

5. We may do something by _ _ _ _ _ _ _ _.

6. It is not always _ _ _ _ to choose to love like Jesus.

Now write the letters from the ◯s above to complete this sentence.

God gives us the gift of ◯◯◯◯◯◯ .
　　　　　　　　　　　　　　1　2　3　4　5　6

How will you use God's gift today?

2 Following God's Law

Do you think rules and laws are important? Tell why.

Tell about some rules and laws that you have to follow. How do they help you?

What would your family, your school, or your community be like without them?

Tell what might happen if . . .
- you played with the computer all night.
- there were no traffic lights.
- you could talk in class anytime you wanted.

Tell what might happen if . . .
- everyone obeyed the recycling rules.
- children never played with matches.
- everyone were treated fairly.

14

Write what rule or law you might see on signs in these places.

* at a railroad crossing
* in a library
* at a zoo park

Tell why these are good rules.

Because God loves us so much, He gives us laws to help us. Why do God's people need rules and laws? Share your ideas.

Let's pray.

†Dear God, teach us Your law. Help us to follow it.

The Most Important Law

What if someone asked you to name the most important law of all? What would you say?

One day someone asked Jesus just that question.

"Teacher," he said to Jesus, "which is the greatest commandment that God gave us?"

Jesus answered,

"The greatest commandment is this:
Love the Lord your God with all your heart,
with all your soul, and with all your mind.
Love your neighbor as you love yourself."

Based on Matthew 22: 35–39

We call this greatest commandment the Law of Love.

Jesus said that the most important law is love — love of God, love of others, and love of ourselves. When we obey this great Law of Love, we do what God wants us to do.

Let's say the Law of Love together.
Can you learn it by heart?

God's Law

We show that we love God, others, and ourselves when we follow the Ten Commandments. They help us to live the Law of Love, as Jesus did.

The Ten Commandments tell us how God wants us to show our love. Sometimes people choose not to follow God's law. They turn away from God's love. They sin.

Sin is freely choosing to do what we know to be wrong. It means disobeying God's law on purpose. All sins are wrong.

Sin hurts us and hurts the members of God's family, too. When we sin, we choose not to love God or others or ourselves. Even when we sin, God does not stop loving us. God always forgives us when we are sorry and try not to sin again.

Look at page 19 to learn how the Ten Commandments teach us to love as God wants.

Third Commandment

18

Living the Ten Commandments

We show we love God when:

1. We think first of what God wants when we make choices.

2. We use God's name only with love and respect.

3. We keep Sunday as God's special day of prayer and rest.

We show we love ourselves and others when:

4. We listen to and obey those who care for us.

5. We care for all living things.

6. We respect our own bodies and the bodies of others.

7. We do not take anything that is not ours; we are fair to everyone.

8. We are truthful in what we say and do.

9. We are faithful to those we love.

10. We help people to have what they need to live.

Fifth Commandment

Fourth Commandment

Doing What God Wants

Draw a 😊 beside the sentences that tell how to follow God's commandments.

Draw a ☹ beside the sentences that do not tell about following God's laws.

○ When I make a choice, I think only of what I want.

○ I keep Sunday as a special day to pray to God with my parish at Mass.

○ I listen to and follow what my parents tell me.

○ I am unkind to people I don't like.

○ I ask to use my friend's bike to go to the park.

○ I will keep God's commandments today by
_____.

Gather in a prayer circle. Have ten people read in turn one of the sentences on page 19. After each one, pray together:

✝ Loving God, help us to do what is right.

At Home

Talk with your family about the ways you will try to live the Law of Love this week.

Cut out the Law of Love pinwheel in the back of the book.

Read the message on the pinwheel. Share it with your family. Then use the pinwheel as a centerpiece for your family table.

heart, mind, and soul.

as yourself.

Love others

Love God with all your

Family Focus

In this lesson your child explored the Law of Love and the Ten Commandments as the laws God has given us to help us live as He wants us to live. You might want to begin by discussing together some family rules and how they help your family. Then talk about God's laws. Emphasize that God gives us laws to help us live healthy and happy lives.

Note that the Ten Commandments themselves are not given. The children are taught how to live the commandments. They are worded in such a way that young children can understand and relate to them. If you wish to review the commandments, see page 19. (You can find the scriptural wording in Exodus 20:1–17.)

1. Have your child tell you the gospel story of the greatest commandment. Go over the Law of Love together. Then go over the explanations of the Ten Commandments on page 19.

2. Help your child understand that sin is a free choice to do what we know is wrong. We cannot sin if we do not choose to do so. Make sure your child knows that God always forgives us when we are sorry.

3. Do the **At Home** activity together.

21

3

Being Sorry, Being Forgiven

Ben and Tony had a fight. They called each other bad names. They wanted to hurt each other. Tony's big brother pulled them apart. "Calm down," he said. "This is no way to settle things." Ben and Tony took deep breaths. They calmed down. Then they

How would you end each story? Share with your group.

Laura received a new computer game for her birthday. She brought it to school to show her friends. When Mark saw it, he was jealous. He had wanted one like that for a long time. So he grabbed the game and threw it. Then this is what Mark did.

Janine wore her sister's favorite necklace without asking. Her sister was very upset. She thought the necklace was lost. Janine said, "I'm sorry." Her sister answered,

What do you think God wants us to do when we do something wrong?

The One Who Was Forgiven

In Jesus' time people wore sandals. The roads were very dusty. When guests were invited to someone's house, the host would have a servant wash their feet with water to make them feel comfortable. It was an act of welcome, of courtesy.

One day, Simon, an important man in town, invited Jesus to his house for dinner. Simon, however, did not welcome Jesus with courtesy. He did not offer Jesus water to have His feet washed.

During the dinner, a woman who had committed many sins came in. She knelt at Jesus' feet. She cried so hard that her tears washed the dust from His feet. She wanted Jesus to know how sorry she was for her sins.

Simon was very angry. He said to Jesus, "Don't you know this woman? She is a sinner. You shouldn't let her be near you!"

Jesus said, "Simon, when I came to your house, you gave me no water for my feet. This woman has washed my feet with her tears. I tell you, Simon, all her sins have been forgiven because of her great love."

Then He said to the woman, "Your sins are forgiven. Go in peace."
Based on Luke 7:36–40, 44–50

Why did Jesus forgive the woman? What do you think Jesus wants us to do when we have done something wrong? What does Jesus want us to do when someone does something wrong to us? Why?

Being Sorry, Being Reconciled

Jesus knew that the woman was sorry for all her sins. Jesus understands when we are sorry, too. Like the woman, we will be forgiven, no matter what we have done, when we are sorry.

Sometimes it is not enough just to say "I'm sorry." Being sorry also means wanting to make up, or to be reconciled, with those we have hurt. It means trying not to sin again.

Reconciliation is the sacrament in which we celebrate God's mercy and forgiveness of our sins.

When we celebrate the sacrament of Reconciliation, we tell God that we are sorry for what we have done wrong. We promise not to sin again and to try to make things right. God always forgives us.

We say a special prayer of sorrow when we celebrate Reconciliation. It is called an Act of Contrition. Contrition is sorrow for sin.

Try to learn this Act of Contrition by heart.

An Act of Contrition

My God,
I am sorry for my sins with all my heart.
In choosing to do wrong
and failing to do good,
I have sinned against you
whom I should love above all things.

We tell God we are sorry.

I firmly intend, with your help,
to do penance,
to sin no more,
and to avoid whatever leads me to sin.

We promise not to sin again. We try to make up for our sins.

Our Savior Jesus Christ
suffered and died for us.
In his name, my God, have mercy.

We ask God to forgive us in Jesus' name.

Forgiveness and Peace

Explain to someone what happens in the sacrament of Reconciliation.

Is there someone to whom you need to say "I'm sorry?" Will you? How? Is there someone you need to forgive? Will you? How?

Listen to this song, then sing it. It tells about God's forgiveness. (To the tune of "Joyful, Joyful!")

Jesus, Jesus, please forgive us,
For the times we did not love.
We will try to be disciples,
And spread peace and joy to all.
Thank You, God, for Your forgiveness
For our failings and our sins.
We are joyful for God's blessings,
Helping us to love again.

Pray the Act of Contrition. Then sing the song together.

At Home

When we have done something wrong, we say:

"Please _____ me."

When a person has hurt us, we say:

"I _____ you." We have learned that when we are sorry, God will always _____ us.

Find the word by coloring only the "x" spaces.

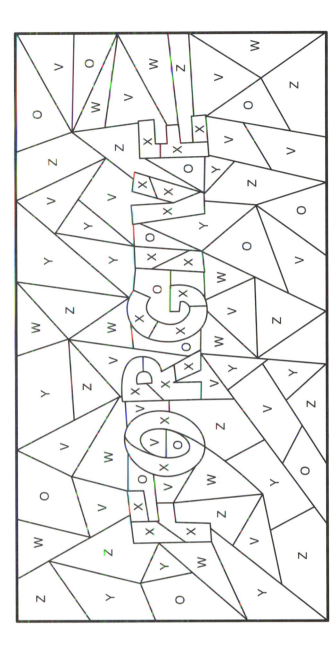

Pray the Our Father together with your family. Listen carefully for this word as you pray.

Family Focus

The Church teaches that the sacrament of Reconciliation brings about in us wonderful effects:

- reconciliation with God and the Church
- remission of eternal punishment incurred by mortal sin
- peace of conscience; interior joy
- increase of spiritual strength. (See *Catechism*, 1496.).

In this lesson your child learned about forgiveness. Ask your child what it means to say, "I'm sorry."

1. Then read through the opening stories together to see how well your child understands that being sorry for a sin may require more than words. We must make up with the person who has been hurt. We must promise not to sin again.

2. Invite your child to tell you the story of the woman Jesus forgave. Ask your child *why* Jesus forgave her.

3. In the sacrament of Reconciliation, we pray a special prayer of sorrow called an Act of Contrition. Help your child learn this prayer by heart. There are several acts of contrition that can be said. We are suggesting your child learn this one by heart.

4 Examination of Conscience

Sit in a circle. As everyone sings the song, one child walks around the circle and taps someone on the shoulder. That person stands up and joins the circle and taps someone on the shoulder. That person stands up and joins hands with the child outside the circle. The second child taps another who then joins the outside circle.

Sing the song (to the tune of "Go Round and Round the Village") until everyone is standing up holding hands.

♪ Go round and round God's love ring,
Go round and round God's love ring,
Go round and round God's love ring,
And find someone who cares. ♪

Talk about what it means to belong to God's love ring.
How do you know when you are living God's love?

Sometimes it is easy to tell right from wrong.
Sometimes it is hard to know the best
choices we should make.
What do you do to make good choices?
What questions do you ask?
What people help you?

Make up a prayer asking the Holy Spirit to
guide you. Share your prayer with a friend.

Jesus wanted us to know how much God
loves and cares for us — even when we do
things that are wrong. Here is a story He told.

The Lost Sheep

Once there was a shepherd who had one hundred sheep. He cared for all of them. One day one of the sheep got lost. The shepherd was so worried about the lost sheep that he left all the others to go and look for it.

After a long search, the shepherd found the lost sheep. He picked it up gently and carried it home on his shoulders.

The shepherd was full of joy. He called to his friends, "Come, and celebrate! I have found my lost sheep."

Then Jesus told the people that there is great joy in heaven when a sinner is truly sorry.
Based on Luke 15:4–7

Jesus is our Good Shepherd. He loves and cares for us. When we do what is wrong and are truly sorry, He is full of joy.

We Know Right from Wrong

In the story Jesus told, the lost sheep did not know it was doing something wrong.

People are different from sheep. We can know whether our choices are good or bad. We call this way of knowing right from wrong our conscience. Conscience helps us to know what is right and what is wrong.

Before we celebrate the sacrament of Reconciliation, we ask God the Holy Spirit to help us remember our sins. This is called an examination of conscience.

We think about the times we made a bad choice, or did what was wrong. We also remember the times we should have done good things but did not. We ask ourselves whether we have been living as Jesus wants us to live.

Here are some questions to help you to examine your conscience.

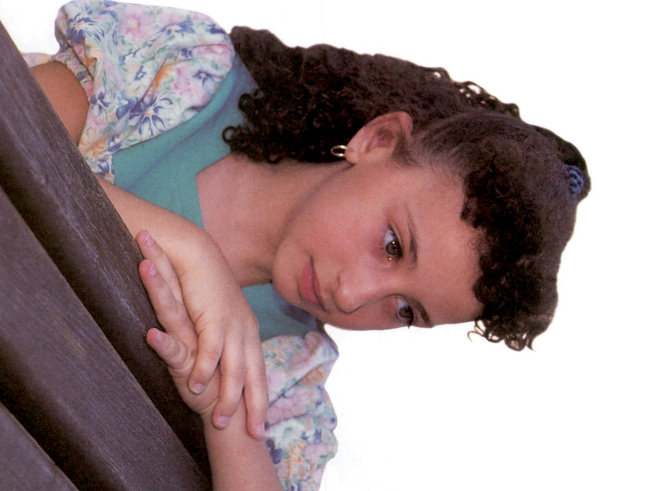

An Examination of Conscience

1. When I make choices, do I sometimes forget to think first about what God wants me to do? Have I done what God wants?

2. Have I used the name of God or Jesus in a bad way?

3. Did I worship God at Mass each Sunday?

4. Have I disobeyed the grown-ups who take care of me?

5. Have I been angry with or cruel to others?

6. Have I forgotten to show respect for my body and the bodies of others?

7. Have I taken anything that is not mine or treated others unfairly?

8. Have I always told the truth?

9. Have I hurt someone by what I have said or done? Have I been jealous of others?

10. Have I refused to help people who are in need? Have I been selfish?

The Good Shepherd

Act out the story of the lost sheep with your friends. Show how you think the sheep felt when it was lost, and how it felt to be found. How did the shepherd feel when he found and carried his sheep home?

Now be very still. Listen to the music. Then sing the song as a prayer to end your lesson.

Always Ready to Forgive
Carey Landry

♪ You are always ready to forgive, O Lord, always ready to forgive. When we come to you with sorrow in our hearts, you are always ready to forgive.

Like a shepherd searching for a lamb that has strayed, looking and searching ev'rywhere. When he finds that lamb he takes her in his arms; he embraces her and carries her home. ♪

At Home

Help the shepherd find the lost sheep. Use a crayon or marker.

After you help the shepherd find the lost sheep, pray this prayer with your family.

✝ Jesus, You are our Good Shepherd. You guide and protect us. Help us always to make loving choices. Amen.

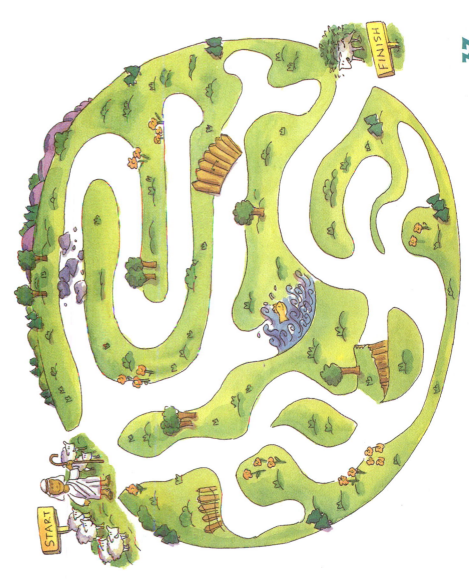

Family Focus

This lesson on examination of conscience is a very important one for young children. It should be presented in the context of the love and care God has for them especially as expressed, at least in part, in the love and care they experience at home and in the faith community. We do not want our children to become guilt-ridden or scrupulous. Yet we must help them become aware of their responsibilities as baptized members of the Church. We also want to help them to become aware of the great love and mercy of Christ, who supports them when they do what is right and who forgives them when they do what is wrong.

Conscience is that awareness we have about the rightness or wrongness of our choices. In young children it should be developed gently and consistently.

1. Read through the lesson together. Invite your child to tell you the story of the lost sheep. Ask how we are like the lost sheep when we do what is wrong.

2. Go over the questions for an examination of conscience on page 35. Your child might want to suggest other or different questions. You might want to add ones that you find helpful.

3. Pray together the words of the song your child learned on page 36. Then help your child do the **At Home** activity.

5

Celebrating Reconciliation

Act out this gospel play together.

Reader 1: A man named Zacchaeus lived in the town of Jericho. He was a tax collector and a very rich man. The people of the town did not like him because he had cheated them.

One day Jesus was going to Jericho. A large crowd had gathered to see Him. Zacchaeus also wanted to see Jesus. But Zacchaeus could not see over the people's heads because he was short.

Zacchaeus: I can't see Jesus! I know what I'll do. I'll climb up this tree.

Reader 2: So Zacchaeus climbed the tree. Soon Jesus came by. He looked up and said,

Jesus: Zacchaeus, come down quickly! I want to stay at your house today.

Reader 3: Zacchaeus jumped down. He was so happy! Jesus wanted to stay at *his* house.

All: (grumbling) Jesus is going to stay at the house of this tax collector. Zacchaeus is a sinner. He cheated us.

Zacchaeus: Jesus, I am sorry I have done wrong things. I am going to give half of all I have to the poor. If I have cheated anyone, I promise to give back four times what I owe.

Reader 4: Jesus knew Zacchaeus was truly sorry for his sins. Jesus forgave Zacchaeus. He said,

Jesus: Today, Zacchaeus, I bring you forgiveness and peace.

All: (To the tune of "Did You Ever See a Lassie?")
♫Oh, we are friends of Jesus, our Brother
  and Shepherd.
Jesus teaches us to love and to follow
  His way.
Our friends and our family will help us
  get ready.
For Your peace and Your forgiveness,
  dear Jesus, we pray. ♫

Why do you think Jesus forgave Zacchaeus?
Why do you think Jesus forgives us?

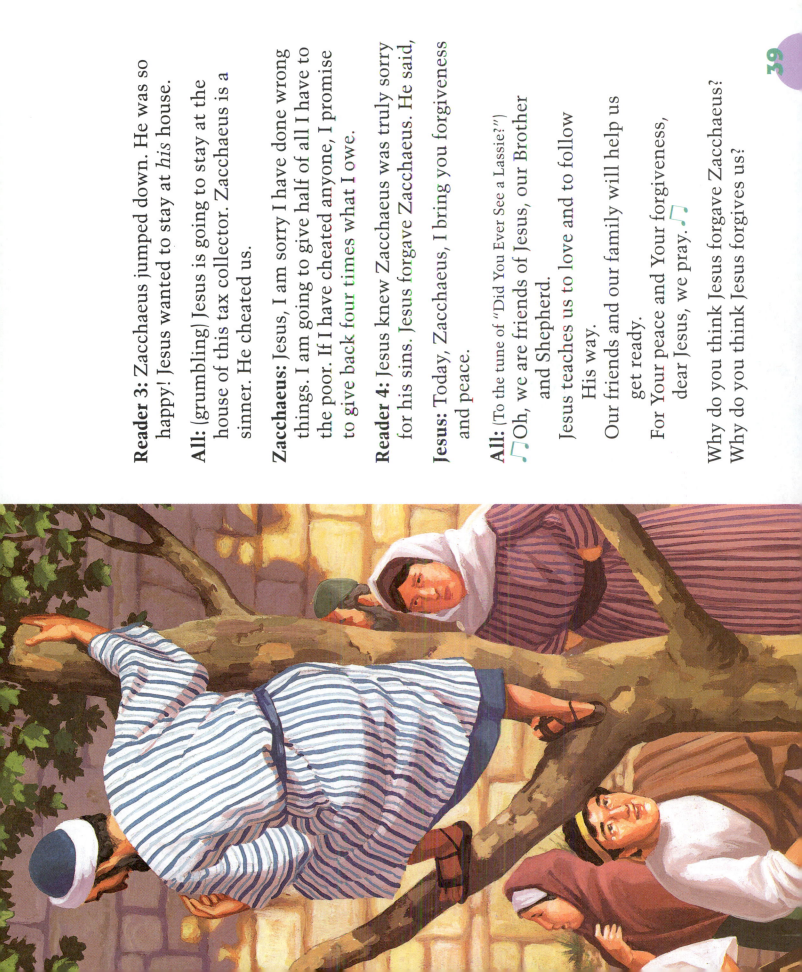

The Sacrament of Peace

Jesus shares with us God's forgiveness and peace in a special way in the sacrament of Reconciliation. He forgives our sins. Jesus makes us one again with Him and with the Church.

Jesus gave His apostles the power to forgive sins in His name. Jesus said to them, "Receive the Holy Spirit. Whose sins you shall forgive will be forgiven." By the power of the Holy Spirit, the priest continues the work of the apostles. He forgives sins in Jesus' name, too.

We can celebrate the sacrament of Reconciliation in two ways. We can celebrate the sacrament *alone* with the priest. Or we can also celebrate the sacrament *together* with the priest and our parish family.

In each of these celebrations, we go one by one to talk to the priest. We can talk to him face-to-face or from behind a screen. We tell our sins to God by telling them to the priest. This is called making our *confession.*

In both ways of celebrating Reconciliation, we tell God we are sorry for our sins. We promise not to sin again. God forgives us, and we are at peace with God and one another.

Individual Rite of Reconciliation

When we celebrate Reconciliation by ourselves with the priest, this is what we do.

- We get ready to celebrate the sacrament by making an examination of conscience.

- We go into the reconciliation room to meet with the priest. He greets us in God's name and in the name of the Church. We make the sign of the cross together.

- We listen. The priest may read a story to us from the Bible about God's love and forgiveness.

- We confess our sins to God. We do this by telling our sins to the priest. The priest will never tell anyone what we say in confession!

- The priest helps us remember how Jesus wants us to love God and one another. We promise not to sin again. The priest then gives us a penance. A *penance* is a prayer or good work we do to show God we are sorry.

- We pray an act of contrition. We promise to try not to sin again.

- The priest says the words of absolution. He forgives our sins in the name of the Father, and of the Son, and of the Holy Spirit. *Absolution* means that our sins are forgiven.

- We thank God because our sins have been forgiven in this wonderful sacrament.

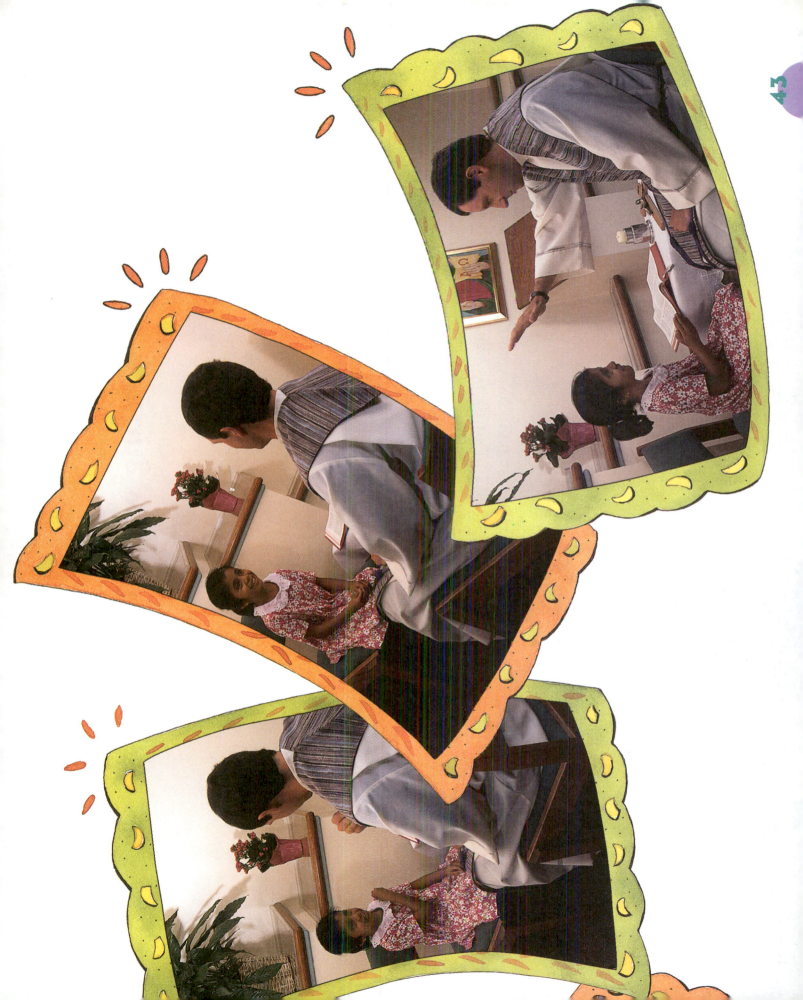

Celebrating with Others

When we celebrate the sacrament of Reconciliation with the priest and with other people in our parish, here is what we do.

* We gather with our parish family and sing a song. The priest welcomes us in the name of the whole Church.

* We listen to a story from the Bible about God's mercy. The priest or deacon explains the story. He reminds us that God always loves us and that God forgives us when we are sorry for our sins.

* We examine our conscience. We think about the times we may not have lived as followers of Jesus.

* Together we pray an act of contrition and the Our Father. We ask God to help us not to sin again.

* The priest meets with us one by one. We make our confession. Remember, the priest never tells anyone what we say to him!

* The priest gives us a penance.

* Then the priest says the words of absolution. This means that our sins are forgiven.

* After all have had a turn to meet with the priest alone for confession, we gather together again.

Celebrating Reconciliation

These steps are always part of the celebration of the sacrament of Reconciliation.

- We examine our conscience and are sorry for our sins. We promise not to sin again.

- We confess our sins to the priest.

- We receive a penance.

- We pray an act of contrition.

- The priest gives us absolution, and we thank God for His mercy.

- We thank God because our sins have been forgiven. We are sure that we are God's friends.

- The priest blesses us. He asks us to bring Jesus' peace to others.

- We sing a song to thank God for forgiving us.

We Prepare

With your group, visit the reconciliation room in your parish church. Talk about the things you see there. Choose the way you would like to receive the sacrament.

Share together your thoughts and feelings about celebrating the sacrament of Reconciliation for the first time.

What else will you do to prepare to celebrate this wonderful sacrament of God's peace?

Cut out the heart in the back of the book. Pray the prayer. Attach a ribbon to the heart and place it around your neck. Then sing *My First Reconciliation Song* together.

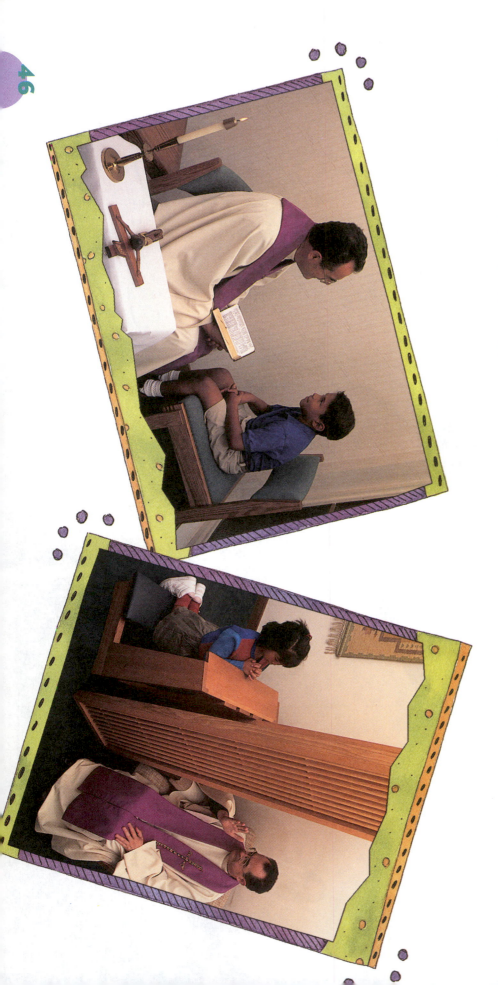

 At Home

The choices we make affect everyone around us, especially the members of our families. Our loving choices help us to grow. Make a "Loving Choices Tree" like the one below for your family.

Draw a branch for each family member. When someone makes a loving choice, add a leaf to that person's branch.

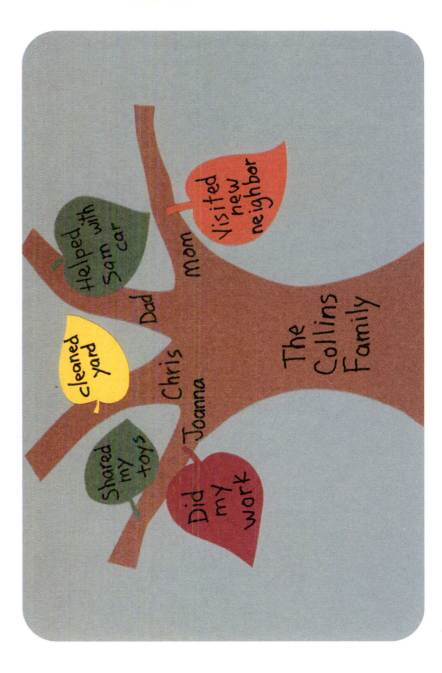

Helped with Sam's car

cleaned yard

Visited new neighbor

Shared my toys

Did my work

Dad

Mom

Chris

Joanna

The Collins Family

Family Focus

1. In this lesson your child has been introduced to two ways we celebrate the sacrament of Reconciliation: by ourselves with the priest and together with the priest and the community.

Your child may be a little confused or nervous about what will happen at First Reconciliation. Go over the lesson slowly and confidently. This will help your child to look forward to this new milestone.

1. Invite family members to take part in the opening gospel play. Then read through the lesson together. Help your child come to a beginning understanding of the *communal* effects of sin. Because we are united to one another in Christ, the loving or unloving choices we make affect the whole community.

2. Gently take your child through the steps of the celebration. Encourage your child to choose the way he or she is most comfortable in celebrating the sacrament. Review the Act of Contrition with your child. See page 27.

3. Summarize by going over the five simple steps on page 45.

4. Invite the whole family to take part in the **At Home** activity.

6

Living as Peacemakers

Gather in a circle. Be very still as you look at the picture. Imagine that you are one of the children in this Bible story.

Let Them Come to Me

One day some mothers and fathers brought their children to Jesus. They wanted Jesus to lay His hands on the children and bless them.

Jesus had been teaching the people all day. There was a crowd all around Him. The disciples saw the children and their parents trying to reach Jesus. They stopped them.

"Take the children away," the disciples said. "Jesus is too busy."

Jesus said, "No, do not send them away." He called the children to Him. He put His hands on their heads and blessed them.

Jesus loved children very much. He said to His disciples,

"Let the children come to Me and do not stop them. The kingdom of God belongs to children like these."

Based on Mark 10:13–16

Imagine you are one of the children close to Jesus. What do you say to Him? What does He say to you? How do you feel? What will you do?

After Reconciliation

We should try to celebrate the sacrament of Reconciliation often. We celebrate it especially to prepare for important times in the Church year such as Christmas and Easter.

When we celebrate the sacrament of Reconciliation, we are like the children with Jesus. He doesn't want anything to keep us from being with Him. He wants us to be filled with His peace. We are friends with Jesus. We are at peace with ourselves and with all God's people.

Jesus wants us to share His peace with our families, with our parish community, and with everyone we meet.

Parish Pancake Breakfast

How to Bring Peace to Others

We can:

- live the Law of Love and the Ten Commandments.

- be thankful for God's forgiveness and forgive others.

- be kind and loving members of the Church both at home and at school.

- try to help those who are not being treated justly or kindly.

How can you bring the peace of Jesus to someone today?

Saint Francis of Assisi was a great peacemaker. His special prayer will remind you of ways you can share the peace of Jesus with others. Join together to pray his prayer.

Prayer of Saint Francis

Lord, make me an instrument of Your peace:
where there is hatred, let me sow love;
where there is injury, pardon;
where there is doubt, faith;
where there is despair, hope;
where there is darkness, light;
where there is sadness, joy.

52

t **Home**

How can you share the peace of Christ with others?

Make a circle of peace to hang near your front door. On one side print the words "Christ's Peace to All." On the other side find pictures that show peace. You can use family photos that show peaceful times.

1. Cut out two circles of the same size.

2. After decorating the circles glue them back-to-back.

3. Punch a hole at the top. Put a string through to use as a hanger.

Family Focus

Congratulations! You have been a good shepherd to your First Reconciliation child. In preparing your child for this healing sacrament, you have been a minister of reconciliation and peace. Continue to encourage your child, in word and example, to have a positive attitude toward this sacrament of God's mercy. It is most important to help your child to become comfortable with the sacrament by celebrating it often.

This closing lesson is a very important part of your child's understanding that the sacrament lives on in us as we go forth to obey the Law of Love, to honor the Ten Commandments, to act justly, and to make peace with others.

Begin this session by embracing your child and thanking him or her for being so faithful in preparing for First Reconciliation.

1. Invite your child to tell you the story of Jesus and the children. Share the follow-up questions.

2. Talk about what we do as Jesus' peacemakers after we celebrate the sacrament. Then pray together the prayer of Saint Francis on page 52.

3. Help your child to do the **At Home** activity.

A Peacemaking Rite

Child 1: Our parish family is rejoicing with us. We have celebrated the sacrament of Reconciliation for the first time. Jesus has given us His healing gift of peace. Jesus said, "Peace I leave you, My peace I give to you." Let us share with one another a sign of God's peace.

Now let us join together in prayer and thanksgiving.

Child 2: For the gift of God's peace given to us in the sacrament of Reconciliation,

All: Jesus, we thank You.

Child 3: For the help of our family and friends,

All: Jesus, we thank You.

Child 4: For teaching us to share love and peace with others,

All: Jesus, we thank You.

Leader: Parents, you have prepared your children to celebrate this wonderful sacrament of mercy and forgiveness.

When your child's name is called, please come forward with your child to receive the certificate.

Now let us join hands and pray the prayer that helps us to be peacemakers: Our Father….

Let There Be Peace on Earth
Sy Miller and Jill Jackson

♫ Let there be peace on earth
And let it begin with me.
Let there be peace on earth
A peace that was meant to be.

With God as our Father
We are family.
Let us walk now together
In perfect harmony.

Let peace begin with me;
Let this be the moment now.
With every step I take
Let this be my solemn vow:
To take each moment and
Live each moment
In peace eternally.
Let there be peace on earth
And let it begin with me! ♫

Begin

with Me!

Summary: I Will Remember

1. What is the Law of Love?

The Law of Love is "You must love God with all your heart. You must love others as you love yourself."

2. What are the Ten Commandments?

The Ten Commandments are laws that tell us what God wants us to do. They help us to live healthy and happy lives.

3. What is sin?

Sin is freely choosing to do what we know to be wrong. It means disobeying God's law on purpose.

4. What is the sacrament of Reconciliation?

Reconciliation is the sacrament in which we celebrate God's mercy and forgiveness of our sins.

5. What steps are always part of the sacrament of Reconciliation?

We examine our conscience; we confess our sins; we receive a penance; we pray an act of contrition; we receive absolution.

6. What do we do after Reconciliation?

After Reconciliation, we share the peace of Jesus with our families, our parish community, and with everyone we meet.

1 Preparing for Reconciliation

Jesus, help us to make good and loving choices.

I am preparing to celebrate Reconciliation

1. Jesus helps us to make good and loving

   _____.

2. To make a right choice, we begin by asking

   the _____ to help us.

3. Mistakes and accidents are not

   _____.

FOLD

I remember God's word

Show how the son found his way home. Color the stones as you choose the correct words to fill in the story.

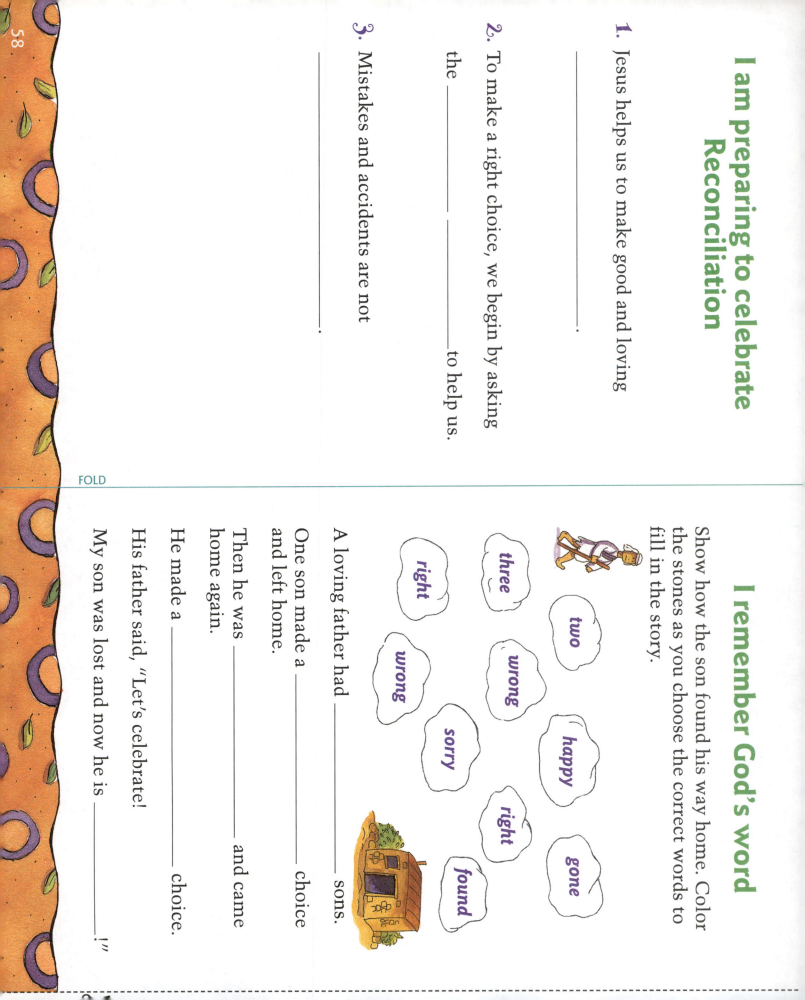

two

three   wrong

right   happy

wrong   right

sorry   gone

found

A loving father had _____ sons.

One son made a _____ choice and left home.

Then he was _____ and came home again.

He made a _____ choice.

His father said, "Let's celebrate!

My son was lost and now he is _____!"

Loving God, You always forgive us when we are sorry.

I am preparing to celebrate Reconciliation

1. When we love God, others, and ourselves we are living the _____ of _____.

2. Freely choosing to do what we know is wrong is _____.

3. The _____ tell us what God wants us to do to show our love.

FOLD

I remember God's word

Jesus said the greatest commandment is:

Love the Lord your God with all your heart,
^{8} ^{6} ^{2}

with all your soul, and with all your mind.
^{4} ^{3}

Love your neighbor as you love yourself.
^{1} ^{9} ^{7} ^{5}

What do we call this greatest commandment? Use the numbered letters above to find the answer.

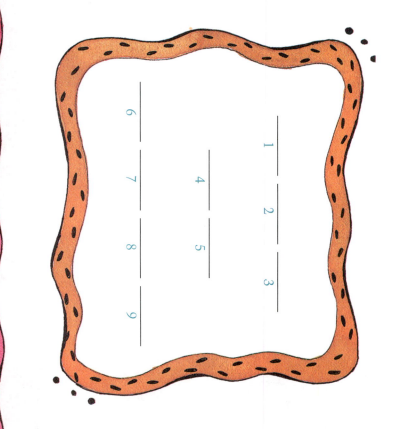

___ ___ ___
1   2   3

___ ___ ___
4   5

___ ___ ___
6   7   8   9

3 Preparing for Reconciliation

Thank You, Jesus, for joy, forgiveness, and peace!

I am preparing to celebrate Reconciliation

1. Jesus forgives us, no matter what we have done, when we are _____.

2. Being sorry means making up, or being _____, with those we have hurt.

3. A special prayer of sorrow is called the _____ of _____.

FOLD

I remember God's word

Finish the Bible story. Write the words in the puzzle.

One day Jesus was invited to Simon's house for dinner. A woman who was a sinner came in.

1. She was _____ for her sins.

2. Jesus forgave her because of her great _____.

3. He said, "Your sins are _____."

4. Go in _____."

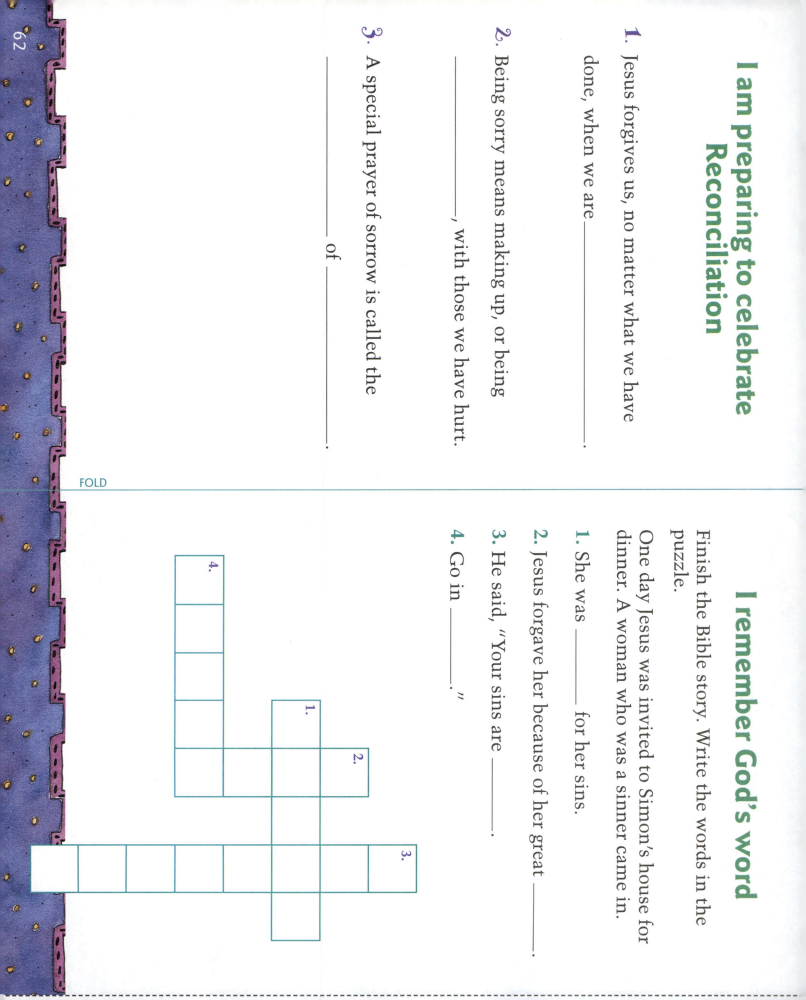

4 Preparing for Reconciliation

J esus,
our
Good Shepherd,
You find us
if we are lost.
You gently
lead us
back home.
Jesus,
Your love
and care
never ends.

I am preparing to celebrate Reconciliation

1. Our _____ tells us when we are not loving God or others.

2. We ask the _____ to help us think about the choices we make.

3. When we ask ourselves whether we have been living as Jesus wants we our _____.

FOLD

I remember God's word

Tell why Jesus is like the shepherd in the story of the lost sheep.

_____
_____
_____
_____
_____
_____
_____

5 Preparing for Reconciliation

Jesus,
bless my
heart
to
know
Your love!

I am preparing to celebrate Reconciliation

1. Jesus gave His disciples the power to

_____ in

His name.

2. Telling our sins to God by telling them to the priest is making our _____ .

3. A prayer or good work to show we are sorry is a _____ .

I remember God's word

Unscramble the letters to complete each sentence. Then read the Bible story.

Zacchaeus wanted to see _____ .
                  sesJu

Zacchaeus was so _____ he climbed a tree.
           rhsto

Jesus stopped and talked to _____ .
             hcaZcsuea

Zacchaeus felt _____ for cheating people.
           yrosr

Zacchaeus _____ to give back
          mpdoesri
anything he had taken.

Jesus _____ Zacchaeus because he
      gefrova
was truly sorry.

What does Jesus want us to do when we have done something wrong?

FOLD

6 Preparing for Reconciliation

Lord, make me an instrument of Your peace!

I am preparing to celebrate Reconciliation

1. Jesus wants us to share His _____ with everyone.

2. We bring peace to others when we live God's _____ of _____.

3. When we need forgiveness we should celebrate the sacrament of _____ .

FOLD

I remember God's word

Complete each sentence. Then find and circle your answers in the letter box.

One day some mothers and fathers brought their _____ to Jesus.

They wanted Jesus to _____ their children.

The disciples said, "Take the children _____ ."

Jesus is too _____ ."

Jesus said, "No! Let the children _____

to _____ ."

```
C X O C J L P T
O R U H M Q M E
M S A I S B C D
E N B L E S S S
P B Q D O U I E
Z U Y R A W A Y
O S A E R T W N
A Y C N K J D S
```

Celebrating Reconciliation with Others

We sing an opening hymn and the priest greets us. The priest prays an opening prayer.

We listen to a reading from the Bible and a homily.

We examine our conscience.
We make an act of contrition.

We may say a prayer or sing a song, and then pray the Our Father.

We confess our sins to the priest. In the name of God and the Christian community, the priest gives us a penance and absolution.

We pray as we conclude our celebration. The priest blesses us, and we go in the peace and joy of Christ.

Celebrating Reconciliation by Myself

The priest greets me.
I make the sign of the cross.
The priest asks me to trust in God's mercy.

He or I may read a story from the Bible.

I talk with the priest about myself.
I confess my sins: what I did wrong and why.
The priest talks to me about loving God and others.
He gives me a penance.

I make an act of contrition.
In the name of God and the Church,
the priest gives me absolution. (He may extend or
place his hands on my head.)
This means that God has forgiven my sins.

Together, the priest and I give thanks
for God's forgiveness.

Prayers

Our Father

Our Father, who art in heaven,
hallowed be thy name;
thy kingdom come;
thy will be done on earth
as it is in heaven.
Give us this day our daily bread;
and forgive us our trespasses
as we forgive those
who trespass against us;
and lead us not into temptation,
but deliver us from evil.
Amen.

Hail Mary

Hail Mary, full of grace,
the Lord is with you;
blessed are you among women,
and blessed is the fruit of your
womb, Jesus.
Holy Mary, Mother of God,
pray for us sinners now
and at the hour of our death.
Amen.

Glory to the Father

Glory to the Father,
and to the Son,
and to the Holy Spirit:
as it was in the beginning,
is now, and will be for ever.
Amen.

Morning Offering

My God, I offer You today
all I think and do and say,
uniting it with what was done
on earth by Jesus Christ,
Your Son.

Evening Prayer

Dear God, before I sleep I want
to thank You for this day so
full of Your kindness and Your joy.
I close my eyes to rest safe
in Your loving care.

Prayers

Prayer of Quiet

Sit in a comfortable position.
Relax by breathing in and out.
Shut out all sights and sounds.
Each time you breathe in and
out, say the name "Jesus."

Based on Psalm 8:9

Psalm of Praise

O God,
Your greatness is seen in all
    the world.

Based on Psalm 8:9

Psalm of Sorrow

Remember, God, Your
    kindness and constant love.
Forgive my sins.

Based on Psalm 25:6–7

Psalm of Thanksgiving

I thank You, God, with all
    my heart.
I sing praises to You.

Based on Psalm 138:1

Psalm of Trust

May Your constant love
    be with us, O God,
as we put our hope in You.

Based on Psalm 33:22

Psalm for Help

Remember me, O God, when
    You help Your people.

Based on Psalm 106:4

Act of Contrition

See page 27.

A Peacemaker Checklist

Here is a checklist to help you and your family keep on the "right track" to peace. Each time you follow the road to peace, draw a happy face in the circle. Together help one another to live as God's peacemakers.

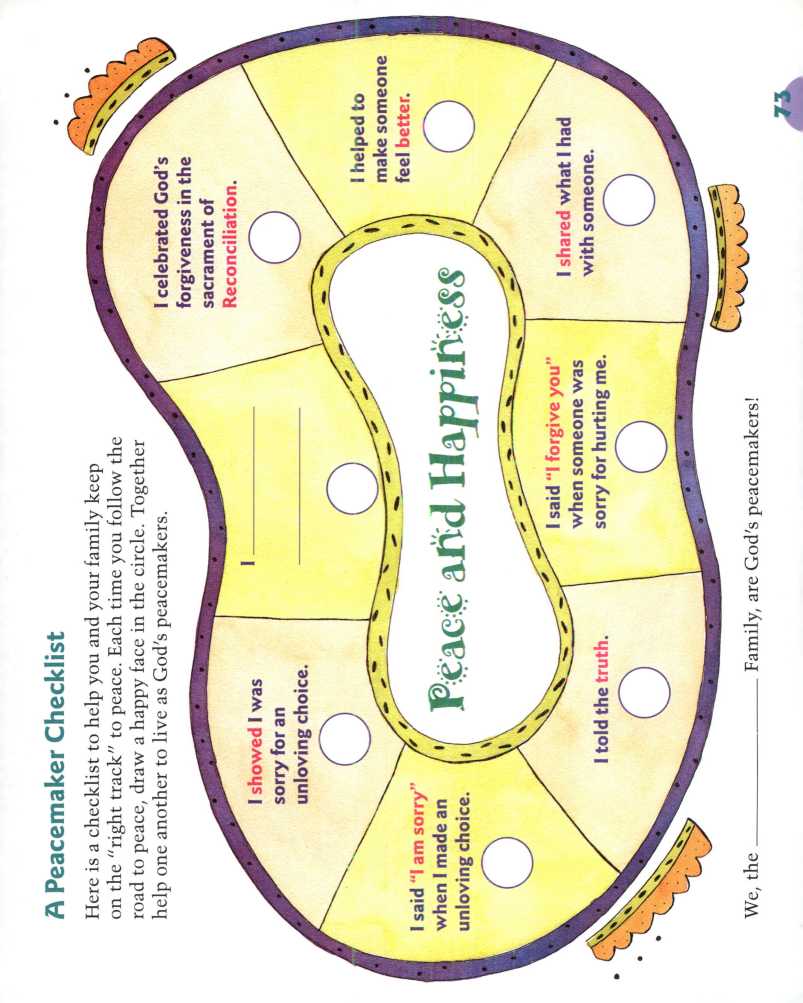

Peace and Happiness

I celebrated God's forgiveness in the sacrament of Reconciliation.

I helped to make someone feel better.

I shared what I had with someone.

I said "I forgive you" when someone was sorry for hurting me.

I _____

I showed I was sorry for an unloving choice.

I said "I am sorry" when I made an unloving choice.

I told the truth.

We, the _____ Family, are God's peacemakers!

Being God's Peacemakers

Think of another way that you live as God's peacemakers.

Write it in the space on the track.

Now carefully cut on the broken line.

Hang your peacemaker checklist in a special place.

Make time during the week to go over the checklist with your family.

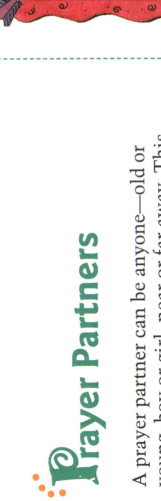

Prayer Partners

A prayer partner can be anyone—old or young, boy or girl, near or far away. This person is special. As you prepare to receive God's gift of forgiveness in Reconciliation, your prayer partner helps you. He or she remembers you in thought and prayer.

Ask your teacher for the name of a home-bound person or a person in a nursing home. You can also help this person. By asking him or her to become your prayer partner, you will help this person feel needed and special.

Complete the letter on this page. Remember to put your name. You can add your own special message, too. Then carefully cut on the broken lines to send your message.

Dear _____,

I am so excited!

I am getting ready to receive the sacrament of Reconciliation.

There are so many new things I have to _____.

I need your help.

Will you be my prayer partner?

Your _____ will help me during this special time. I want to grow in my faith like you.

Love,

_____

An Invitation

An Invitation

You are being asked to
support this young person with
your "prayer and care"
during these weeks of preparation
for the sacrament of Reconciliation.

We hope that
you will join with us
at this special time.

More Songs for Reconciliation

God Has Made Us a Family

Carey Landry

(can be used with Chapter 2)

God has made us a family and together
we will grow in love.
God has made us a family and together
we will grow in love.

1. Oh, Yes! We need one another,
as together we grow in love;
and we will forgive one another,
as together we grow in love.

2. We will reach out to those in need,
as we learn to grow in love;
to those who are lonely and hurting,
as we learn to grow in love.

We Come to Ask Forgiveness

Carey Landry

(can be used with Chapter 3)

We come to ask your forgiveness, O Lord,
and we seek forgiveness from each other.
Sometimes we build up walls instead of
bridges to peace,
and we ask your forgiveness, O Lord.

1. Sometimes we hurt by what we do to
others. Sometimes we hurt with words
that are untrue. Sometimes we cause
others pain by what we fail to do and we
ask your forgiveness, O Lord.

2. For the time when we've been rude and
selfish; for the times when we have been
unkind; and for the times we refused to
help our friends in need, we ask your
forgiveness, O Lord.

More Songs for Reconciliation

New Hope

Carey Landry

(can be used with Chapter 5)

1. New hope, new hope is what we have
   been given by the Lord;
   new hope, new hope is what we have
   been given by the Lord. **

** Alleluia, Alleluia, Alleluia, Lord;
   Alleluia, Alleluia, Alleluia, Lord.

2. New life, new life is what we have
   been given by the Lord;
   new life, new life is what we have
   been given by the Lord. **

3. A new heart, a new heart is what we have
   been given by the Lord;
   A new heart, a new heart is what we have
   been given by the Lord. **

Peace to You and Me

Carey Landry

(can be used with Chapter 6)

Peace to you; peace to me;
peace to each of us.
From me to you and you to me,
we bring the gift of peace.

1. The peace that we live;
   the peace that we give is
   the peace of Christ.
   In giving forgiveness,
   love and care, we share the
   gift of peace.

2. From one to one, then
   on and on, we share the
   gift of peace. From all who
   give to all who receive,
   we share the gift of peace.

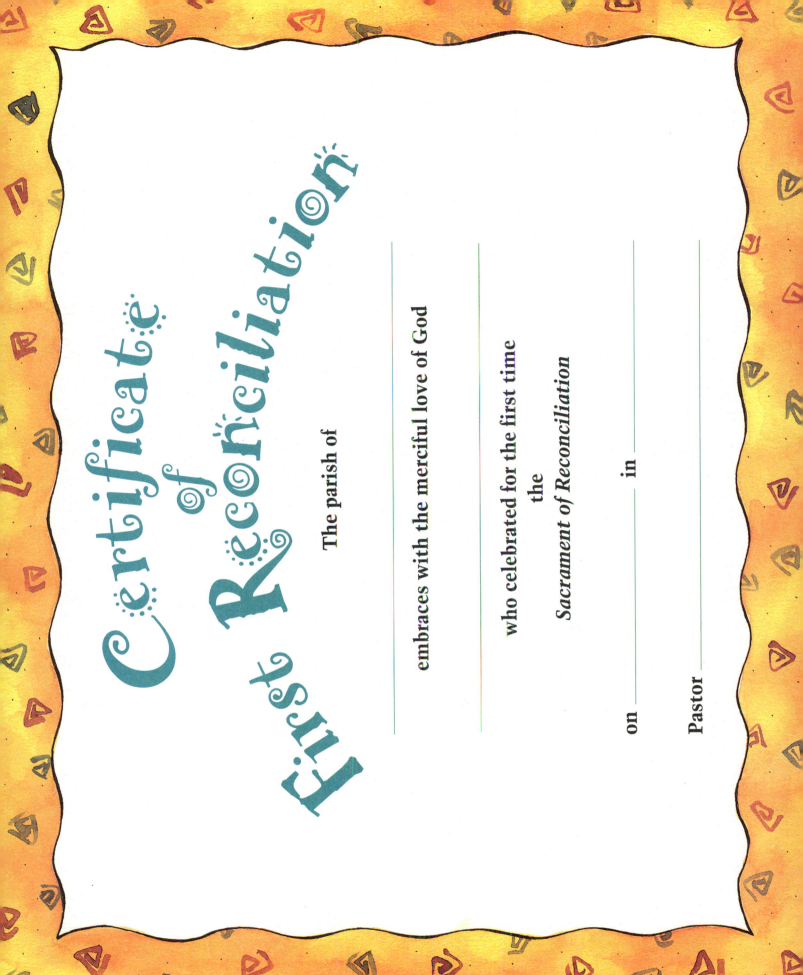

Certificate of First Reconciliation

The parish of

_____

embraces with the merciful love of God

_____

who celebrated for the first time

the

Sacrament of Reconciliation

on _____ in _____

Pastor _____

fold
fold